IMAGES
of America

CAMP VERDE

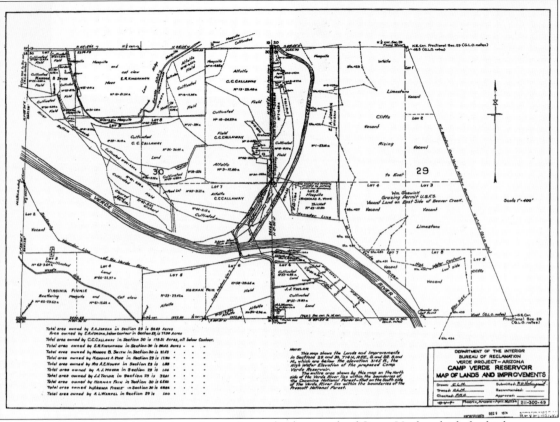

In 1934, the Bureau of Reclamation engineered a dam south of Camp Verde, which, had it been built, would have put most of the community underwater. This map is one of 38 drawn by surveyor Fritz Holmquist, showing the improvements to properties the government would have been forced to purchase. The maps provide a rare snapshot of what Camp Verde and the surrounding area looked like in the winter of 1933–1934. (Courtesy Camp Verde Historical Society.)

ON THE COVER: Fort Verde so impressed Martha Summerhayes, the wife of U.S. Army quartermaster corps officer Lieutenant Jack Summerhayes, that she sung its praises in the famous memoir of her trip through Arizona in 1874, *Vanishing Arizona*. On arriving at Fort Verde after a weary and dangerous trip from Fort Apache, she wrote, "Here are lace curtained windows, well-dressed women, smart uniforms, and, in fact, civilization compared with what we had left." (Courtesy Arizona State Parks.)

IMAGES
of America

CAMP VERDE

Steve Ayers and the
Camp Verde Historical Society

ARCADIA
PUBLISHING

Copyright © 2010 by Steve Ayers and the Camp Verde Historical Society
ISBN 978-0-7385-7912-2

Published by Arcadia Publishing
Charleston, South Carolina

Printed in the United States of America

Library of Congress Control Number: 2010926121

For all general information, please contact Arcadia Publishing:
Telephone 843-853-2070
Fax 843-853-0044
E-mail sales@arcadiapublishing.com
For customer service and orders:
Toll-Free 1-888-313-2665

Visit us on the Internet at www.arcadiapublishing.com

To all of those who have kept Camp Verde's story alive

CONTENTS

ACKNOWLEDGMENTS

In 2004, I started working as a reporter for Verde Valley Newspapers, publishers of the *Verde Independent* in Cottonwood and *The Bugle* newspaper in Camp Verde. Working out of the Camp Verde office, I soon began taking an interest in the valley's history. The job has given me the opportunity to explore the valley's past in ways not open to others, for which I am deeply grateful.

In 2009, after pestering the many wonderful volunteers at the Camp Verde Historical Society for information and occasionally helping repatriate their files with documents and information found elsewhere, I was asked to join their board of directors.

It is to the Camp Verde Historical Society that I give the real acknowledgment for having made this book possible. I extend a special thanks to Babs Monroe and Ernestine Murdock, whose personal memories helped fill the void left by written records. I also wish to thank society member Ron Brattain who endured hours scanning photographs.

The information in this book comes from a host of original archives as well as several books that have captured Camp Verde's past, not the least of which is *Pioneer Stories of Arizona's Verde Valley*, first published by the Verde Valley Pioneers Association in 1933. Its collection of first hand accounts is indispensable. I must also acknowledge the significant collection of historical accounts written by journalists, local historians, and others over the years.

Last and certainly not least, I would like to thank Arizona State Parks for their generosity in sharing Fort Verde's photographic collection, along with their continued protection of the old fort.

Unless otherwise noted, all images are courtesy of the Camp Verde Historical Society and Arizona State Parks.

INTRODUCTION

In 1583, about 24 years before the founding of Jamestown, a Spanish conquistador named Antonio Espejo traveled from the Hopi pueblo of Awatovi to the Verde Valley in search of gold mines. His journey may have taken him down Beaver Creek and on to the Verde River. Where he and the handful of men he traveled with crossed these two streams is unknown, but we can assume that their journey took them through what are today the town limits of Camp Verde.

A chronicler of Espejo's trip, Diego Perez de Luxan, dismissed the mines as worthless, "as they were copper mines and poor." Little did Espejo or his men realize, they were standing over one of the richest deposits of gold, silver, and copper in the American Southwest—deposits that would one day give birth to the mines of Jerome and provide a thriving market for a group of farmers who had made their homes near where the Spanish gold seekers had crossed the river.

The community of Camp Verde traces its roots to another gold strike, this one about 50 miles west in the mountains surrounding the present-day community of Prescott. Believing the placer gold found in Granite Creek, Big Bug Creek, and Lynx Creek was just a taste of the mineral wealth buried in the mountains of central Arizona, the miners soon found their way east to the Verde Valley.

These early prospectors never found the gold they sought. Instead they found the homeland of the Yavapai and Apache people, a broad valley with many flowing streams and hillsides littered with the stone pueblos and other remnants of a long lost civilization.

In January 1865, despite the dangers of settling in Indian country, a group of nine men from Prescott came to the Verde Valley, checking out reports of rich farmland. Along with 10 others, they returned a month later. Half of them went upstream to carve out a home on the banks of the Verde River. Half went downstream to the banks of West Clear Creek. The half that went upriver left within three months, having unsuccessfully attempted to dig an irrigation ditch from the Verde River. The group that settled on West Clear Creek built a fort from the crumbled remains of one of the ancient Indian pueblos, dug an irrigation ditch from the gentle and reliable West Clear Creek, and by May, had 200 acres under cultivation.

No sooner was the farm thriving than the Indians, who had previously left them unmolested, began raiding the farm. According to one account, the settlers' losses by mid-summer amounted to several bushels of corn every night, not to mention the occasional head of livestock.

Despite their numerous pleas for military protection, it was not until August 1865 that help arrived. The soldiers spent the first four months camped near the settlers' farm. In January 1866, they moved 4 miles upriver to the confluence of Beaver Creek. By 1872, the soldiers had established a permanent fort on high ground between the two previous sites, providing protection for the nearly 300 people living along the river and its tributaries.

The war between the whites and the Indians cost hundreds of lives. The vast majority of them, however, were Yavapai and Apache. The war was a slowly evolving battle of attrition until fall 1872, when, under the leadership of Gen. George Crook, the soldiers took the upper hand. By keeping the Yavapai and Apache bands on the run throughout winter 1872–1873, Crook and his soldiers effectively starved them into submission. By spring 1873, over 2,000 Indians had surrendered to the inevitable and were forced to live on the Rio Verde Reservation.

But in many people's eyes, promises made to Indians meant nothing. In February 1875, despite Crook's objections, 1,473 Yavapai and Apache were herded out of the Verde Valley and driven across some of the state's most rugged country to a desolate reservation at San Carlos, 180 miles away, where most would remain for the next 25 years.

With the Indian problem mitigated, white settlers began homesteading the former 900-square-mile reservation, building farms, mining the mineral wealth of the Black Hills, and building a new life.

Several attempts were made to turn the 9,000-acre Fort Verde Military Reservation, the center of the town of Camp Verde today, into an Indian reservation when the military announced it was vacating the fort in 1890. However, objections from the whites living in the area put an end to the idea. By 1899, the entire military property had been homesteaded or sold at auction, and the town of Camp Verde began taking shape.

Twelve years later, the population of Camp Verde briefly swelled when speculators began touting the Verde Valley as the next West Texas. A veritable sea of oil lay beneath, they said, just waiting to be tapped. But as quick as the oil frenzy began, it came to an end. Several locals also tried over the years to find the elusive mother lode of mineral wealth, said to lay somewhere within the Cherry and Squaw Peak mining districts on the outskirts of town. Once again, the promise never materialized.

The town enjoyed a brief period of prosperity when an ancient salt deposit, mined by the Sinagua Indians some 700 years earlier, was tapped once again in 1923. The mine employed 100 men and shipped 130 tons a day before foreign competition forced its closure in 1933.

In 1911, Camp Verde became one of the first communities in the state to enact prohibition by popular vote, nearly eight years before the rest of the nation. Later it would become the hub for a network of moonshiners who took advantage of the valley's remoteness, its ample supply of water, and its considerable population of thirsty cowboys and miners.

From around 1910 to approximately 1930, the farmers, ranchers, and residents of Camp Verde endured a constant haze of acrid smoke generated by the smelters in Jerome, Clarkdale, and Clemenceau. The smoke took a heavy toll on orchards, farm fields, and grasslands, while generating many lawsuits.

In the 1930s, most of what is today the town of Camp Verde nearly drowned beneath a reservoir that would have provided water and power for the metropolitan Phoenix area. Fortunately the plan was stopped at the last minute when the federal government declared the project too expensive.

Isolated much of it life, the town and its hardy residents have managed to hang on, through two world wars, the Great Depression, and the whims of the modern world. Throughout its history, Camp Verde has remained a community built on hard work and close ties to friends and neighbors. Incorporated in 1986, the town now boasts a population of nearly 12,000, living the life they want in a place they have chosen.

One

THE INDIANS

When the original settlers arrived in the Verde Valley, they were aware they were establishing a community in the homeland of two tribes with a history of intolerance for outsiders.

The Yavapai, a Yuman-speaking people, and the Northern Tonto Apache, an Athabaskan-speaking people, had coexisted, intermarried, and lived along the Verde River and its tributaries for over 300 years. Essentially nomadic, they roamed, farmed, and hunted what is now central Arizona.

Their rapport with outsiders began on a peaceful note when, in 1583, Spanish conquistador Antonio Espejo became the first European to see the Verde Valley. In search of riches, the Yavapai and Apache fed him and his men, gave offerings of peace, and led them to what would one day become the copper mines of Jerome.

Over time though, abuses by the Spanish military and their complicit clergy, along with civilian intrusions into Indian lands and slave raids, destroyed that relationship. The arrival of Anglo-American miners in 1863 only exacerbated a preexisting conflict.

The Yavapai and Apache's hit-and-run war with the settlers began shortly after the Indians realized that white farms were an easy source of corn and cows. Soon though, their battle turned to one of survival as the military and a cadre of Indian scouts hunted them relentlessly. By spring 1873, most of the Yavapai and Apache in the Verde Valley had surrendered to their pursuers and taken up a white man's life on a 900-square-mile reservation.

But in winter 1875, they were forced to leave the Verde Valley and marched 180 miles south through high mountains, winter snows, and swollen rivers to the San Carlos Reservation. There they would remain until families began wandering back around the turn of the 20th century.

Over the last century, they have recovered only a fraction of the land that was once theirs. Through it all, they have preserved their culture and managed to turn Indian gaming into a financial engine that is bringing them gradually to prosperity.

Armed with little more than bows, arrows, and stone tools, the Yavapai and Apache living on the Verde River in the 1860s were ill equipped to confront the coming storm. For over three centuries, they had managed to hold their own—first against the Spaniards, who showed little inclination to enter their rugged homeland and then against the Mexicans, whose brief claim to land north of the Gila River was little more than lines on a map. But Anglo Americans heading west after the Civil War did what the Spaniards and Mexicans could not do in 250 years—uproot them from their homes and nearly destroy their culture, in the brief span of 10 years.

The Yavapai and Apache were resourceful warriors. It did not take them long to learn the ways of their enemy. When equipped with modern firearms, they proved to be a formidable foe. The total number of Anglos who died in the fight has never been tallied. The first soldier to die on the Verde, Pvt. Joseph Fisher, was killed on February 27, 1864, a year before the military established its first garrison in the Verde Valley. In spring 1892, shortly after the fort closed, a train of wagons brought the bodies of 52 soldiers from the Camp Lincoln cemetery to Prescott's Fort Whipple.

The Yavapai were a Yuman-language-speaking people, tied in history and tradition to other "Pai" tribes, including the Havasupi, Hualapai, and the Paipai. The Apache spoke an Athabaskan language, common to the Navajo and tribes living in Canada, Alaska, and the northern Great Plains. On the Verde, the two tribes lived side by side, intermarried, and were, after 1700, increasingly bilingual. Whites typically referred to the Yavapai and Apache of the Verde Valley as either Tonto Apaches or Mohave Apaches.

Always moving with the seasons, the Yavapai and Apache both adopted the practice of carrying their children in cradleboards. Made of bent wood, reeds, fibers, and hide; often decorated with beads or other ornaments; and lined with rabbit fur, cradleboards served as most children's crib, car seat, and playpen for the first year of their life. The carrier allowed the women to work with their hands and carry out their daily chores while keeping the child situated in a manner that kept their backs straight and exercised their neck muscles. The cradleboard also gave the child an opportunity to be visually stimulated by their environment while safe and secure.

Referred to as one of the "Dandy Scouts" by Gen. George Crook, Quatha-Hooa-Hooba, or Yellow Face, served with the 5th Cavalry at Fort Verde, Fort McDowell, and Fort Grant, as a scout. He was reputed to have been a swift runner capable of covering 60 miles across rough country in five hours.

An army scout for 27 years and a tribal policeman for seven more, Captain Smiley was a well-respected leader of his people. During his years as a scout he participated in the surrender of Geronimo and led troops from Fort Verde to Big Dry Wash, the scene of the last major confrontation between Apache and the army in central Arizona. He died in 1936, at age 103. (Courtesy of the Yavapai-Apache Nation.)

Many Yavapai and Apache enlisted as scouts for the U.S. Army. This picture shows five of them. Rowdy, on the far left, was awarded the Congressional Medal of Honor in 1890 for bravery in the Indian wars. He died in a brothel in Miami, Arizona, in 1893 when the proprietor shot him in the back with a shotgun. He was buried at Fort Grant on March 28, 1893, and was eventually reinterred at Santa Fe, New Mexico. Second from the left is Upside-down Charlie, so named because of his insistence on wearing his army belt buckle upside down. Next to him is The-Ho-Anna. On the far right is Yellow Face, the famous runner.

This is a posed photograph of Company C of the Apache Scouts. As an Indian Scout, the men were allowed a degree of freedom not enjoyed by those forced to live on the reservation. Some Indians, however, scorned them as turncoats.

This photograph of Company B of the Indian scouts at Fort Verde was taken between 1875 and 1879, after much of the battle for the Verde Valley was over. Following the surrender of hundreds of Yavapai and Apache after the winter campaign of 1872–1873, many joined the army for the pay and adventure it afforded rather than submit to reservation life.

16

Mickey Free, stepson of southern Arizona rancher John Ward, was born Felix Telles before he was captured by Apache Indians in 1861, when he was 13 years old. He became an Apache warrior and eventually an Apache scout. Stationed at Fort Verde from December 1874 to May 1878, Free served as an interpreter.

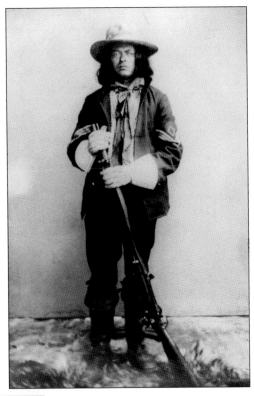

Al Sieber, seated in the center of the first row, was a scout who was both respected and detested by the Indians he led and those he hunted down while stationed at Fort Verde. In 1875, he was among the contingent of soldiers and civilians who escorted the Yavapai and Apache out of the Verde Valley, on their expulsion to San Carlos. In 1908, while working with an Indian crew at Roosevelt Dam, he was crushed to death by a rock.

The Apache used hunting masks like this one while stalking their prey, a practice that allowed them to get close enough to kill with a bow and arrow. Chief Cha' Lii Pa'h (Gray Hat), known to the whites as Charlie Pan, gave this one to Dr. William Corbusier, medical doctor on the Rio Verde Reservation. It was reported that not long after the soldiers arrived, most of the game in the valley had been taken and what survived was so spooked it took a rifle to kill it. Cha-lipan became chief of scouts under Gen. George Crook at Fort Verde after he surrendered at Fort Verde in 1873 along with 250 followers.

Apache women, pictured here, wore two-piece camp dresses with a separate skirt and top. Yavapai women wore one-piece dresses. They both wore their traditional dresses long after the men had taken to wearing shirts, jeans, and cowboy hats. Both cultures were matrilineal, meaning they considered themselves to be either Apache or Yavapai based on their mother's tribal affiliation.

By the early 1900s, when the Yavapai and Apache began returning to the Verde Valley, all the tillable land had been settled by white families, leaving them to settle on either marginal land or take up residence on, and work for, a local farm or ranch.

By 1872, following seven years of attrition, 1,700 Dilzhe'e (Tonto) Apache and Yavapai were on the Rio Verde Reservation. In April 1873, 1,000 Yavapai from the Camp Date Creek Reservation east of Prescott joined them.

It was not until 1937, about the time this photograph was taken at the Camp Verde Reservation, that the Yavapai and Apache became recognized as a sovereign tribe by the U.S. government and began to establish a legal hold on their former homeland.

The first Indian school in the Verde Valley was established in 1907 in Fort Verde's former administration building—the same building that now houses the park's museum. Indian children were not permitted to attend white schools until the 1940s.

This photograph taken in 1909 shows the students and staff of the first reservation school. The Anglo couple to the right of the post is Angie Gabbard and her husband Taylor Price Gabbard. Taylor Gabbard served as superintendent of the Camp Verde Apache Indian Agency and was a staunch advocate for the reestablishment of Indian lands. The Gabbard family left Camp Verde in 1915, eventually moving to Tempe, Arizona.

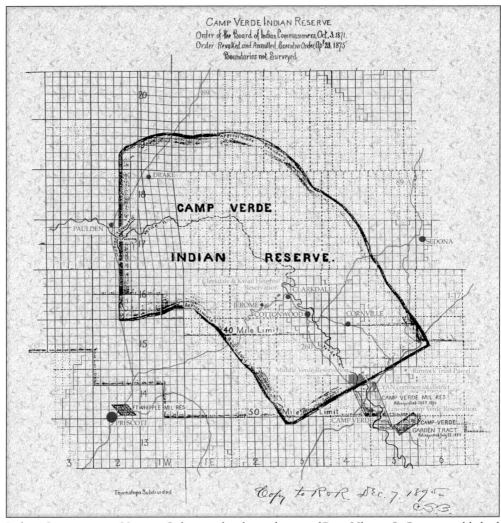

Indian Commissioner Vincent Colyer, under the authority of Pres. Ulysses S. Grant, established the Camp Verde Reservation, a 900-square-mile allotment for the Yavapai-Apache people, in 1871. It included a 10-mile-wide strip on each side of the Verde River for 45 miles and included the land on which the communities of Cottonwood, Clarkdale, and Jerome were later established, along with the mineral deposits that later fed the valley's economy. In 1875, following pressure from government contractors in Tucson, President Grant abolished the reservation. (Courtesy of the Yavapai-Apache Nation.)

Two

THE SETTLERS

Of the men and women who came from Prescott to settle the Verde Valley in the winter of 1865, we know the names of several thanks to the account of James Swetnam.

Clayton Ralston, Henry D. Morse, Jake Ramstein, Thomas Ruff, James Parrish, James Robinson, John Lang, Charles Yates, John Culbertson, William Osborn, Ed and Lois Boblett, Joe Melvin, Polk James, James Sanford, a Mr. and Mrs. Whitcomb, and a man by the name of "Elliot" from Texas, with a wife and "four or five kids," all appear in Swetnam's account.

By the end of the first year, virtually all of them had left, to be replaced by a heartier lot, willing to endure the hardships. That heartier breed included folks like Wales Arnold, whose ranch on Beaver Creek became a sanctuary for many of the surrounding families when Indian battles flared.

George Hance and his brother John also showed up about that time, as did William "Boss" Head, who took over as the fort's suttler. Joe Marr, D. C. Robinson, Dudley Brooks, H. T. Williams, Poker Johnson, Bill Duncan, the Wingfield clan (including William Gilmore and James Henry) soon arrived along with John Hicks, L. S. Noles, Tom Wartel, and L. M. Olden.

Parson James Bristow would preach the first protestant sermon beneath a cottonwood tree in 1875, several years before he was ordained a minister.

Soon names like Harbeson, Strahan, Mahan, Boyer, Stephens, Marksberry, Casner, Ketcherside, Crane, Fain, Monroe, Murdock, Dickinson, Dickison, Goddard, and Van Daren were added to the census roles.

Descendants of many of these pioneer families still call Camp Verde home. Many of their names also endure as local landmarks or on street signs. Virtually all of them have a brief history on file at the Camp Verde Historical Society, to satisfy the occasional descendant seeking a glimpse into their family's past.

King Woolsey became the first homesteader in Yavapai County when he built a ranch on the Aqua Fria River, 35 miles west of Camp Verde. Repeated Indian raids on his livestock led to at least four retaliatory raids to the Indian homelands in the Verde Valley in 1864. He was once quoted as saying he "fought on the broad platform of extermination" as far as Indians were concerned. It was the reports from Woolsey's expeditions to the Verde that led the first group of adventurers to settle along the banks of West Clear Creek. Woolsey and the men he traveled with were also responsible for returning with the first accounts of Montezuma Well and for naming it and many other local landmarks. After serving four terms in the state legislature, twice as speaker, he died in 1879 at the age of 47, one of the state's wealthiest citizens.

Lured by the rich bottomland along the Verde River, James M. Swetnam was one of the leaders of the first party of settlers. In spite of that, he did not stay long. By 1866, he was on his way back to Colorado where he began studying medicine. Swetnam went on to receive a medical degree in Michigan and practiced in Missouri and Kentucky. It is because of Swetnam's account, written years later when he retired to Phoenix, that there exists an accurate account of the first year's trials and tribulations suffered by those who settled the Verde Valley. (Graphic courtesy Verde Valley Newspapers.)

Shortly after Wales Arnold was honorably discharged at Fort Whipple in August 1864, he set his sights on the Verde Valley. He established a ranch on Beaver Creek, grew hay, and eventually ended up with the contract as the suttler at Camp Lincoln. He and his wife, Sarah, lived in and around Camp Verde most of their lives. Arnold served for a time as a justice of the peace in Beaver Creek.

Wales Arnold's ranch, which included Montezuma Well, was a fortress often used by fellow settlers when the threat of Indian attack raised an alarm. It had loopholes in the walls for shooting but no windows, and it had an inside well. Wales and Sarah had no children; however, they raised an Indian girl they named Lulu who had been given to them after she was captured during an Indian raid.

All who knew Sarah Arnold knew her as Auntie Arnold. Described as a short, dumpy, unprepossessing woman who always wore the same style dress, she arrived in Arizona via Cape Horn and San Francisco. Having been forced to defend her ranch single handed on more than one occasion, she was said to have carried a pistol at her side or within easy reach her whole life. Throughout the years, Sarah gained a reputation among area settlers as a kind-hearted and resourceful woman who would ride miles to aid a neighbor. Sarah Arnold died in 1899 and is buried alongside her husband, Wales, in the Clear Creek Cemetery.

When George Hance arrived in the Verde Valley in 1868, he noted, "There are two ranches, two ditches, 200 acres under cultivation and barely a dozen citizens." One of his first jobs was working for the post suttler at the time, Hugo Richards. It was during his employ with Richards that he gained a reputation for honesty and intelligence. Over his lifetime, he served as a justice of the peace and as the town's notary. It is said he served as the de facto mayor of Camp Verde and was once described by a visiting engineer as the "Major Domo [sic]" of the area. His accounts of the local comings and goings were published regularly in the *Prescott* newspapers and serve as some of the only reports of early life in the Verde Valley.

George Hance

George Hance was a colorful figure. As justice of the peace, he swore in witnesses on a thick black copy of "Dana's Mineralogy," instead of a Bible, feeling both books "were of equal importance." Reputed to have been a non-drinker, he fought vociferously against prohibition, believing the government had no business telling a man how to live his life. A happily married man, he nevertheless had a reputation of fondness for young ladies, insisting on kissing the bride at all the weddings he performed. And as far as religion was concerned, he was known as a vocal critic of the hypocrisies he saw carried out both in front of and behind the pulpit. He was a skilled mediator who boasted he had never presided over a civil case—always finding a resolution that would keep the disputing parties out of his courtroom.

William "Boss" Head (left) purchased the suttler's business from Hugo Richards in 1870 and held it until long after the military abandoned the fort. As the owner of the valley's only store for many years, Head was one of the most prominent and respected businessmen in Yavapai County. The Indian boy on the right is believed to be Mickey Free, an Apache Scout and regular customer at Head's store.

William S. [Boss] Head property of Fort Verde

Mickey Free apache scout

James Sanford arrived in the Verde Valley from the Colorado River in March 1865 at the age of 43, one month after the first batch of settlers arrived. Ironically he left his home on the Colorado because of the constant Indian raids. He spent just a year in the Verde Valley before moving back to Prescott where he lived for 24 years, building a sawmill and investing in real estate.

C. C. Calloway came to the Verde in 1882, and later became one of the first farmers to break ground on the land that had once been the Fort Verde Military Reservation. He originally took up residence in Strawberry Valley, 30 miles east, before coming to Camp Verde in 1899, purchasing a 140-acre parcel near the confluence of the Verde River and Beaver Creek for $2,000. Most of the land remains a farm to this day.

Rösch

Atelier
1513 & 1515 Olive St.
St. Louis.

Charlie Calloway once described himself as a "reasonably hard worker." In his younger days, just like many of his fellow cowboys, Calloway never thought twice about riding from summer pastures on the Mogollon Rim to Camp Verde to attend a dance. In those days, dances were one of the great social events and typically went until dawn with a midnight break for dinner. Calloway would live to be 103.

Uncle Jim Hopkins - Luke Hunt - Bill Lowthian - Bill Wingfield - David Jones - Hank Peach - Jim Lazar

This picture taken in the 1880s shows some of the cowboys from the valley's pioneer families. Virtually every family worked a farm or a ranch. Most of the ranchers grazed their cattle in the valley in the winter, then drove their herds up to the top of the Mogollon Rim in the summer. Pictured from left to right are Jim Hopkins, Luke Hunt, Bill Lowthian, Bill Wingfield, David Jones, Hank Peach, and Jim Lazar.

Esler and Belle Monroe were known far and wide for their hospitality. Their parties were such major social events for Camp Verde, they often made the Prescott newspapers. Belle never let anyone leave without first writing a few words in her daybook. Her collection of daybooks are now in the Sharlot Hall Museum in Prescott.

Riley and Rebecca Casner came to the Verde Valley in 1875 with Riley's two small sons from his first marriage. Shortly afterwards, they left to farm on the Gila River, only to return in 1879 and settle on the last piece of land available on Beaver Creek. They planted a large orchard and raised vegetables and livestock. The two scratched out a living trading butter and vegetables at Fort Verde to buy their necessities. Today their ranch is the campus of Southwestern Academy, an international boarding school.

J. C. Bristow preached the first protestant service in the Verde Valley beneath a cottonwood tree on the banks of the Verde River on October 3, 1875. It would, however, be another four years before he was ordained as a Baptist minister. The topic of that first sermon was "So then, every one of us shall give an account of himself unto God." Bristow (right) is pictured here with two other Camp Verde pioneers, Mr. and Mrs. John Ralston.

J. L. MURDOCK,
Water Delivery.
GOOD FOR 10c.

Josiah Murdock moved to the Verde Valley in 1892. After working as a freighter in the mines in New Mexico, he opened up a business hauling water from the Verde River to area homes that had no well. He filled the barrels by hand with a bucket and was known to promote his business by passing out 10¢ discount coupons, a marketing gimmick that placed him well ahead of his time.

William Goddard and Oliver Farley hauled hay to the thriving mining town of Jerome. From the 1890s to the 1950s, most of the farmers and ranchers living around Camp Verde made their living providing fruit and produce to the miners in Jerome.

Beekeeper Lewis Bell came to the Verde Valley in 1888 from Michigan after a disease decimated the hives he tended. The owner of the apiary would go on to pursue his hobby of making fishing lures, eventually founding the Heddon Sporting Goods Company, a brand name that lives on today. Bell answered an ad for a beekeeper in the Verde Valley, met and married the farmer's sister-in-law Jennie Jordan, and raised three sons.

Oliver Benedict was a longtime farmer in Camp Verde who married Edna Gertha Munds, daughter of another pioneer family. Gertha worked as a schoolteacher at Squaw Peak School. Oliver served on the school board and as the supervisor of the Eureka Ditch, one of Camp Verde's larger irrigation companies.

Ed Wingfield first came to the Verde Valley leading 200 head of cattle. Perhaps more importantly, he brought along three sons, two of whom, William Gilmore and James Henry, would figure prominently in the growth of Camp Verde. William became a rancher, landowner, and businessman. William's son, Robert, would go on to build a business empire after Clinton Wingfield, James Henry's son, was murdered. James Henry would also become a prominent rancher, landowner, and the successful bidder for Fort Verde when it was sold at auction. Henry would live a tragic pioneer's life, losing seven of his ten children along with his wife. However, in 1905 he married Hattie Munds, and the two would live happily until his death in 1926.

Three

THE FORT

Summer 1865 was miserable for the settlers on Clear Creek. Constantly harassed by Indians, the tenacious band lived in a stone fort built from the crumbled remains of an ancient Indian pueblo. Despite the near constant pleas to the army at Fort Whipple, they remained on their own until August 27, 1865, when a force of 18 enlisted men and one officer, all New Mexico volunteers, arrived.

The Camp on the Clear Fork of the Rio Verde, as the soldiers' first encampment was known, was the beginning of a 25-year military presence in the Verde Valley and the first of three military installations to serve the civilian populace.

On January 4, 1866, the soldiers moved their post, by then called Camp Lincoln, to a location less than 1 mile upstream from the Verde's confluence with Beaver Creek.

In 1868, Camp Lincoln's name changed to Camp Verde. Four years later, the army moved to a bluff on the west side of the river, about 1 mile downstream and 80 feet above the malaria-ridden Verde River. The new post would grow to 22 buildings, including a hospital, quartermaster's stores, homes for the officers, and barracks for the enlisted men. In 1878, the name changed to Fort Verde, in recognition of its permanence.

The fort closed in April 1891. In 1895, the U.S. Department of the Interior, the agency that had assumed possession of the fort, opened the 18-square-mile Fort Verde Military Reservation that surrounded the fort, to homesteaders. In August 1899, local rancher James Henry Wingfield purchased the post, its remaining buildings, and the 40 acres on which it sat for $700 at auction.

In 1956, through the efforts of Harold and Margaret Hallett, along with many volunteers, the remaining buildings of Fort Verde were saved as a museum. In 1970, the Fort Verde Museum Association sold the fort to the State of Arizona for $1. Arizona State Parks purchased an additional historic building, along with the former parade ground, and turned it into Fort Verde State Historic Park.

The design of some of the buildings at Fort Verde was greatly influenced by the wife of Gen. George Stoneman, commander of the Arizona Military District in the early 1870s and the commander responsible for implementing a permanent building program at Fort Verde. During a trip to France, Mrs. Stoneman became enamored with the "mansard" style of roof, a four-sided gambrel-style hip roof, made popular by 17th-century French architect Francois Mansard. Although it has the advantage of making use of the attic, this design was not ideal for the Arizona desert before the advent of air conditioning. Between 1873 and 1876, three 2-story Mansard-style buildings were constructed. Two of the buildings burned. Only the commanding officer's quarters remains.

Eight years after Fort Verde was abandoned by the military, it was auctioned off. The buyer, rancher James Henry Wingfield, then sold off most of the buildings for $25 to $50 apiece, unofficially becoming the first developer in town. With building materials at a premium, most tore the old buildings down and used the lumber, windows, and doors for other structures. Three of the homes that once comprised officers' row were used as private residences.

In 1875, with the Indians removed to a reservation 180 miles south in San Carlos, Fort Verde became more domesticated. Officers' families had lived on the post prior to that but gained greater freedom to explore the countryside and take pleasure trips on horseback.

There was once a double row of cottonwood trees planted around the fort's parade ground, described by one military officer as "the largest and best kept in the Territory." After a steam pump arrived, water was pumped from the river to a water tank on a hill to the west and gravity fed to all parts of the post. The soldiers also dug a 4-mile-long irrigation ditch that watered an extensive garden. By the time the residents of Camp Verde began restoring the fort in 1956, the old cottonwood trees were dead. They have recently been replanted by Arizona State Parks as part of a minor rebuilding program, which included a new pathway around the parade ground and new parking areas capable of accommodating recreational vehicles.

Along with the officer quarters, Fort Verde had quarters for the surgeon and the non-commissioned officers, along with four enlisted men's barracks, a guardhouse, granary, commissary, hospital, bakery, barns, stables, and even quarters for the fort's laundresses and hospital matron. The military also maintained a school and a library stocked with newspapers and periodicals, although not always up-to-date.

It is unknown when this photograph of the bachelor officers' quarters was taken. The sign on the front of the building indicates it was being used as a business at the time. County records show the buildings at Fort Verde were bought and sold several times and used for a wide variety of purposes including residences, businesses, a school, and a courtroom.

Fort Verde was saved in 1956 thanks to the Camp Verde Improvement Association. The association appointed a committee responsible for restoring the fort, which became the Fort Verde Museum Association. In 1957, the organization held an open house, which soon became the community's largest annual event, Fort Verde Days. After selling the fort to the State of Arizona in 1970, the museum association changed its corporate name to the Camp Verde Historical Society.

By the 1950s, only three of the original homes on "officer's row" were still standing: the commanding officers' quarters (closest), the bachelor officers' quarters (middle), and the surgeon's quarters. Along with the fort's former administrative building, they comprise the four remaining structures at Fort Verde State Historic Park.

One of the few additions made to Fort Verde over the years was the flagpole added in 1973. The pole is made of two pieces of cedar and constructed in the same manner as a ship's mast. Arizona Public Service Company, the local utility company, provided assistance putting the pole in place.

When the State of Arizona acquired Fort Verde from the Fort Verde Museum Association in 1970, they acquired a property that had been lovingly restored by the citizens of Camp Verde. The association was forced to sell due to the rising cost of maintenance and the lack of money to buy the one remaining building and the parade ground.

A remote fort in the heart of very rugged country, Fort Verde was a tough assignment for the wives and families of military personnel. However, to its credit, Fort Verde was located in a spectacular setting that offered an opportunity for discovery and wonder to anyone adventurous enough to travel about the countryside.

This painting on the wall of the museum at Fort Verde shows how officers' row and the parade ground would have looked in the 1880s. Contrary to popular belief, western military forts from that period were not surrounded by stockades. Walls were unnecessary because the Indians had little inclination to attack such a far superior force.

Harold and Margaret Hallett are the couple ultimately responsible for saving Fort Verde. They purchased the former administrative building as a temporary home while they built a new one. When it came time to sell it, they instead sought support for saving it and the other remaining buildings.

A strip of what was once the fort's parade ground served the residents of Camp Verde as a street for many years. Known as Coppinger Street, the road passed in front of officers' row, then dropped down the bluff below the fort and connected with the road up Beaver Creek.

This picture of the fort's hospital is believed to have been the last one taken before it was torn down and packed off to the Soda Springs Ranch, where its lumber was used to build a barn. It is not known who was driving the Stutz Bearcat, but it may have been a visitor to one of the many dude ranches surrounding Camp Verde in the 1930s. The hospital served the fort's soldiers for almost 20 years and the community for an additional 10 years as a school. The foundation, made of large limestone blocks from the surrounding hills, was recently uncovered during the clean up of a former lumberyard.

The heliograph was a relatively new method of communication when, in 1881, Lt. William Glassford arrived at Fort Whipple in Prescott as the newly appointed chief signal officer. Glassford set up his first heliograph, a device that used mirrors to flash signals across long distances, on Bald Mountain (later known as Glassford Hill) behind Fort Whipple. By 1890, the army had heliograph stations on Squaw Peak, above Fort Verde, Baker Butte, another 60 miles east, and at Fort Apache in the White Mountains, effectively linking all the military posts in northern Arizona. The first communication sent via heliograph between Fort Whipple and Fort Verde was on March 15, 1890.

Fort Verde was chosen for a state park because it constituted the most intact military installation from the Indian War period in Arizona. Many of the other major forts, such as Fort Grant, Fort McDowell, and Fort Crittenden had deteriorated or been plundered.

The average garrison at Fort Verde consisted of one company of infantry and one of cavalry, both at 40 percent strength. It would have typically consisted of 6 officers, 1 surgeon, 109 enlisted men, 4 officers' wives, 1 surgeon's wife, 1 hospital matron, 8 enlisted men's wives, 22 children, 42 horses, and 63 mules.

The average tour of duty at Fort Verde was 13 months but varied widely. The longest any unit was stationed was Company H, 6th Cavalry, which remained just over four years. The shortest was the assignment of K Company, 9th Infantry, which stayed just five months. The shortest assignment by any one individual was the personal tour of 1st Lt. Charles Mason, who was at Fort Verde just 25 days.

Describing officers' row, one report noted, "Officers quarters are on the opposite side of the square facing the west and are also three in number. They are frame buildings with 'mansard' roofs and each containing on the first floor one bedroom, one sitting room and one dining room and one kitchen. Upstairs are servant's apartments."

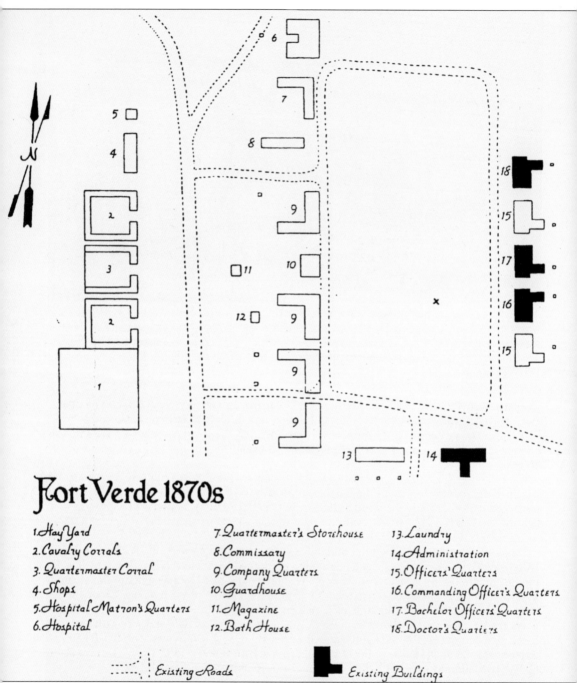

Fort Verde 1870s

1. Hay Yard
2. Cavalry Corrals
3. Quartermaster Corral
4. Shops
5. Hospital Matron's Quarters
6. Hospital

7. Quartermaster's Storehouse
8. Commissary
9. Company Quarters
10. Guardhouse
11. Magazine
12. Bath House

13. Laundry
14. Administration
15. Officers' Quarters
16. Commanding Officer's Quarters
17. Bachelor Officers' Quarters
18. Doctor's Quarters

------- Existing Roads   ▟ Existing Buildings

A medical report from 1873 describes Fort Verde as "Quadrangular in shape. The barracks are constructed of rough boards; with shingle roof: L shaped, and of the following dimensions; Main Bldg. Length 100 ft. breadth 24 feet, height between joints 11 feet. The wing portion measures 76 by 24 feet. The front main building is used as a dormitory, office and storeroom and the wing is used as a mess." The fort had as many as 22 buildings, although because of fire, it is not certain they all stood together at any one time.

50

Four

THE SOLDIERS

On August 27, 1865, Lt. Antonio Abeytia of K Company, 1st Cavalry, New Mexico Volunteers, along with 18 soldiers, a doctor, a wagon, 4 mules, and 30 days rations, arrived on the Verde River near its confluence with West Clear Creek. Answering special order No. 21, Abeytia was instructed to protect a small enclave of white settlers from the Yavapai and Apache, in whose homeland the whites had settled.

It was a miserable existence for the men of K Company, far removed from civilization. It was said that the Indians would not hesitate to attack a party of troops twice the size of a party of settlers or miners because the soldiers did not have the heart, and the settlers and miners were fighting for their lives. Nevertheless, they were a welcome sight and an assurance that the military at last recognized the settlers' presence.

Despite some successes, the units working out of Camp Lincoln were unable to prevail until 1870 when Gen. George Crook assumed command of the Department of Arizona. Crook was a veteran Indian fighter who fought a war of attrition against the Yavapai and Apache. Soldiers were constantly in the field, constantly in pursuit. And aided by Indian scouts, Crook's secret weapon, they finally forced the Indians' surrender in spring 1873.

For the next few years, soldiers from Fort Verde played a game of hide-and-seek with renegade bands that hid out in the hills and canyons rather than submit to reservation life. Their last engagement was at the battle of Big Dry Wash, east of Fort Verde in 1882, when a band of about 60 White Mountain Apaches bolted the San Carlos Reservation and headed north.

Although Gen. George Crook seldom visited Fort Verde, it played an integral role in his 1870s campaign. Once Crook took over, he insisted the soldiers, aided by their Indian scouts, remain in the field at all times, keeping the Indians constantly moving while waging total war, including the destruction of their families and their food stores. In winter 1872–1873, he made life so miserable that by summer 1873, most all of the bands in the area surrounding Fort Verde had surrendered and moved to the Rio Verde Reservation. As aggressive a fighter as he was against the Indians, he was also one of their biggest advocates. He fought a losing battle when the federal government moved to close the reservation and send the Yavapai and Apache to San Carlos.

William Corbusier was one of many doctors who served at Fort Verde. He served during the early 1870s while the Apache and Yavapai were assigned to the 900-square-mile Rio Verde Indian Reservation. His biography, *Verde to San Carlos*, is the only extant record of the Indians' removal to San Carlos in 1875. Corbusier learned the medical profession in California during the gold rush, interpreting for a doctor who did not speak Spanish but nevertheless had a busy practice among the Mexican population.

Capt. Camillo Casatti Cadmus Carr was the commanding officer at Fort Verde from December 1871 to December 1872, during the height of the Indian wars. Carr began his military career as an enlisted man during the Civil War, before being promoted to 1st lieutenant in 1864. Following his service at Fort Verde, Carr advanced to the rank of lieutenant colonel before retiring in 1906.

The blue-eyed, blond-haired Lt. Charles Greenlief Ayres was the commanding officer of the African American 10th Cavalry "Buffalo Soldiers" during their brief stint at Fort Verde. The son of Civil War general Romeyn Beck Ayres, he served at Fort Verde from May 20, 1885, to December 10, 1885, in the company of his wife, Mary Elizabeth Fairfax Ayres. In an odd twist of fate, Elizabeth's father, while serving as staff officer for Confederate general James Longstreet, assaulted a position held by General Ayres, his daughter's future father-in-law, at the Battle of Gettysburg.

Capt. Charles King's claim to fame in life was the publishing of several novels on what it was like to be a soldier on the western frontier. Two of his novels were based on his experiences while stationed at Fort Verde, *The Colonel's Daughter* and *An Apache Princess*. He was wounded during a skirmish at Sunset Pass when a bullet shattered his right arm. He was discharged in 1879. A West Point graduate, King returned to military duty during the Spanish-American War and rose to the rank of brigadier general. His *Colonel's Daughter* character is the inspiration for the title awarded to one young woman each year, who serves as the town's ambassador during Fort Verde Days.

Lt. George Eaton arrived at Fort Verde in December 1873. He served on several scouts along with Al Sieber and Lt. Charles King. King later patterned the hero of his novel *The Colonel's Daughter* after Lt. Eaton. Eaton was instrumental in the creation of the Rio Verde Reservation. After being transferred from Fort Verde he served in the Sioux Campaign in the Black Hills, where he was wounded by the accidental discharge of his pistol during a nighttime horse stampede.

Lt. William Harvey Smith arrived at Fort Verde with Company I, 10th Cavalry "Buffalo Soldiers" in 1885. His records state that he was "casually" assigned to the fort. However, during his casual service he met his wife, Louise Darst Smith, who was visiting her cousin, the wife of another Fort Verde officer, Lt. C. B. McLellan. An accomplished equestrian, Mrs. Smith is said to have fallen in love not only with Lt. Smith but also with the West in general.

Lt. Charles Morton began his military career as an enlisted man. He won the Congressional Medal of Honor at the Battle of Shiloh before attending West Point. He is best known for a scouting expedition he led in 1870, in which his troops fought four engagements against the Apache in a four-day period in the Mazatal Mountains and along the East Verde River. The series of battles resulted in the recapture of 150 horses and mules stolen from ranchers in the Prescott area. He retired as a brigadier general.

Attached to Fort Verde in 1873, Dr. James Reagles is best known for having taken the skull of the Yavapai-Apache leader, Delshay, when he left Fort Verde. Reagles received the head after General Crook paid a $50 bounty on Delshay's head. Reagles's son, Walter, eventually returned the skull to the Fort Verde Museum. It was later repatriated to the Yavapai-Apache people and buried at an undisclosed location.

In the country surrounding Fort Verde, even the cavalry attacked on foot. Two reasons for this were the chronic shortage of horses and the rugged terrain in which the soldiers operated. On average, 65 percent of the soldiers serving at military posts in the Southwest were infantry, not cavalry as portrayed in Hollywood movies.

The soldiers stationed at Fort Verde wore civilian clothing when in the field, a relaxation of military protocol initiated by Gen. George Crook. Understanding the difficulties created by the hot and dry climate, Crook felt comfort trumped military regulation. While in garrison, though, they wore blue wool uniforms.

Gen. George Crook made pack trains a priority, believing rightfully that wheeled supply trains were of little use in the mountains. He was said to have taken pride in his nickname, "Granddaddy of the Pack Mules," even preferring his faithful mule "Apache" to a horse.

Al Sieber was an Anglo scout who was both respected and detested by the Indians while at Fort Verde. In 1875, he was among the small contingent of soldiers and government officials who escorted the Yavapai and Apache out of the Verde Valley on their expulsion to San Carlos. He died in 1908 while working with an Indian crew at Roosevelt Dam, when he was crushed by a rock.

The average private was paid $13 a month, a sergeant $17, and a 2nd lieutenant $116. Officers, however, were responsible for their own expenses. At Fort Verde, the bachelor officers were provided quarters of their own. Alcohol was not allowed on the post and was instead served to the officers in a back room at the suttler's store. Enlisted men wanting a drink frequented a seedy establishment called the Horn Saloon, just outside the southwest boundary of the military reservation.

About 15 miles up the Verde River, on land that was once part of the Rio Verde Reservation, is Peck's Lake. It is named for well-known scout and guide Edmund George Peck, who is said to have lived at the lake, harvesting wild hay and selling it to the military. The lake was a favorite place for soldiers and their families, as well as residents of the area, to picnic and camp.

Hunting was not only a pastime for soldiers assigned to Fort Verde, it was also a means of supplementing the often-inadequate rations delivered by the military. During the fort's early days, all supplies came via steam ships up the Colorado River, then over land by pack train or wagon to Fort Whipple in Prescott. The mountains surrounding Fort Verde were reasonably abundant in game. However, the soldiers' needs often competed with the needs of the Indians. Following the removal of the Yavapai and Apache, hunting camps became a form of recreation, often attended by the officers' wives and their families.

The Buffalo Soldiers played no significant role in the history of Fort Verde. But the unique nature of an all-black regiment fighting Native Americans cannot be ignored. Company I, 10th Cavalry arrived at Fort Verde on May 20, 1885, under Maj. Curwen Boyd McLellen. Major McLellen served as the fort's commanding officer until April 1887. The Buffalo Soldiers remained in garrison until summer 1887 when they were sent to Fern Springs on the Mogollon Rim, a summer camp used by the military to get families and soldiers out of the valley heat. While at Fern Springs, four privates mutinied. Two were acquitted at a court martial. Pvt. James Lee was confined for two months then returned to duty. Pvt. William Johnson was dishonorably discharged and served five years in Leavenworth Prison.

The summer months at Fort Verde were hard on soldiers and civilians alike, with daytime temperatures well in excess of 100 degrees for about four months every year. As a result, the army established summer camps on the Mogollon Rim, north and east of the fort. At 7,000 feet, these camps provided respite for families and convalescing soldiers. This camp was established at Fern Springs, near Baker Butte, in the late 1880s. Families brought along aides, typically enlisted men who were paid an additional stipend for their duties.

Both Montezuma Castle and Montezuma Well were popular picnic spots for soldiers and their families at Fort Verde. The cool shade along Beaver Creek offered a respite from the sweltering summers endured at a time long before the invention of swamp coolers or air conditioners.

Carrie Wilkins was the daughter of Lt. Col. John Wilkins, commander of the 8th Infantry at Fort Verde. A friend of Charles King, Carrie Wilkins became the namesake for King's novel, *The Colonel's Daughter*. In real life, Carrie Wilkins married Capt. Charles Porter, also of the 8th Infantry, after a seven-year courtship. This picture, digitally enhanced from a photograph given to the Fort Verde State Park, depicts Carrie as she looked during the time her family lived in Arizona.

Fort Verde was originally designed as a four-company post with two cavalry and two infantry. The largest complement of soldiers and civilians stationed at any one time included 306 enlisted men, 11 officers, 19 civilians, and 36 Indian scouts. On average, there were 125 troops at Fort Verde at any given time. The lowest troop strength recorded was just before the fort closed, when there were 11 soldiers at the post.

Before Crook arrived on the scene, the only enemy the Indians had to worry about was the whites. After he arrived, they had to worry about other Indians, as his companies of Indian scouts proved to be an effective tool in their pursuit. As this picture shows, Crook was unconventional in many ways, shunning the official uniform and donning a pith helmet and hunting suit when in the field.

Five

THE TOWN

Although Anglo settlers had made their home in the Camp Verde area in 1865, the town did not begin taking shape until just prior to the turn of the 20th century. Before then, the enclave of settlers established in the vicinity of the fort had been known as Lower Verde.

The town of Camp Verde began on the day in August 1899 when the post sold at auction. Prior to that, the only civilian presence on the bluff above the river was the suttler's store.

Within five years, the town boasted two stores, two saloons, a post office, a church, a school, and one "eating house." The *Journal Miner* in Prescott described it as "a wide awake little village."

Soon after, the territorial highway made its way to Camp Verde in 1911, bringing with it the first bridge over the Verde River. In the 1930s, the town dodged a bullet when a last minute decision by the U.S. Department of the Interior denied a proposed dam that would have inundated much of the community and left the downtown area an island in the middle of a 15-mile-long lake.

Along with the copper mines in Jerome, which served as the community's economic engine, the community endured an on-again, off-again economy that lasted until the Jerome mines closed in the early 1950s.

In the 1950s, the Black Canyon Highway, which would later become U.S. Interstate 17, arrived in Camp Verde and with it came an influx of people wanting to escape the bustle of the Phoenix metropolitan area, 90 miles south. Today Camp Verde has a population of nearly 12,000 supported by a broad-based economy, tourism, and retirees.

Prior to 1899, the only civilian building on what is now Camp Verde's Main Street was the suttler's store, which provided items to the soldiers at Fort Verde that the military did not. Built by William "Boss" Head in 1871, it served as the headquarters for Head's many business enterprises, which included farming and ranching on land south of the store. Head, who earned his nickname while serving in the Arizona Territorial Legislature, was the first private citizen to establish his property right within the former reservation.

C. H. Norwood's blacksmith shop was for many years the local garage. It is unknown when he set up shop; however, he is said to have had a reputation as someone who could fix anything, as long as it was made of iron or steel. The building was located just to the north of the stage stop boardinghouse on Main Street.

Joe Crane, owner of a former Fort Verde barracks that became a dance hall, was a life-long bachelor who fancied himself a ladies' man. He was ever ready to kiss a pretty girl, even if she was reluctant. Nevertheless, he was a popular chap and affectionately known to the younger crowd as "Uncle Joe."

The Joe Crane building was originally an enlisted men's barracks at Fort Verde. Later on, it served as a community meeting place and dance hall until it burned down in 1935. Crane lived in an apartment at one end. During the dances, mothers would rest their babies in Joe's apartment.

This street scene from around 1920 shows the dirt path that served as the town's main street until the late 1960s, when it was finally paved. Located in a remote valley some 80 miles north of the prosperous state capital of Phoenix, Camp Verde was visited early on only by those brave enough to drive the twisting mountain roads from Prescott via Cherry Creek Road. In spite of its remoteness, the town served as a crossroads for early travelers coming through northern Arizona.

Lon Mason   Jake Weber   Charlie Norris   Frank Slack   John Fredrick

The Red Star Saloon, owned by Joe Lane, was one of many local saloons that had a precarious existence. The town was a hotbed of the prohibition movement and one of the first communities in Arizona to prohibit the sale of alcohol. After two previous unsuccessful attempts to impose prohibition, the "drys" won an election over the "wets" in 1911. Camp Verde's ban on alcohol predated the rest of Arizona, which went dry in January 1915.

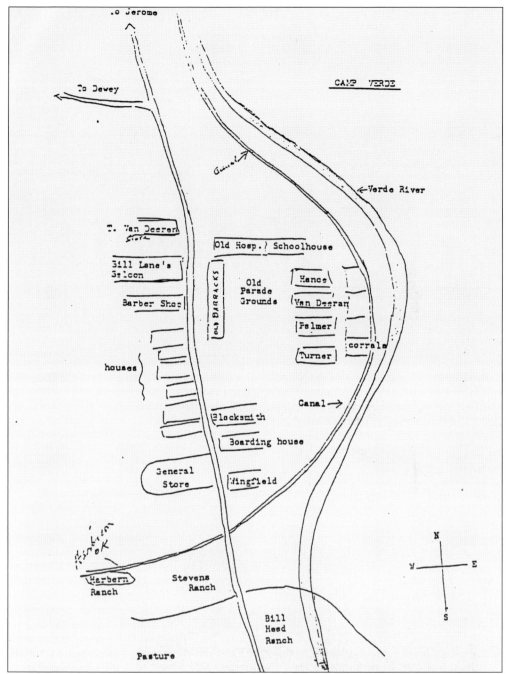

Dr. Ralph Palmer purchased the medical practice of long-time physician Dr. Jim Ketcherside in 1903. Although Palmer was in town barely a year, he produced the only known map of the townsite from that time, showing such noted features as the Wingfield Commercial Company store (general store), Red Star Saloon (Bill Lane Saloon), Joe Crane building (old barracks), Norwood's blacksmith shop, and the schoolhouse when it was located in the old fort hospital. It even notes that George Hance was living in the former surgeon's quarters of the old fort. It does not, however, note that Hance's house served as the community's courtroom.

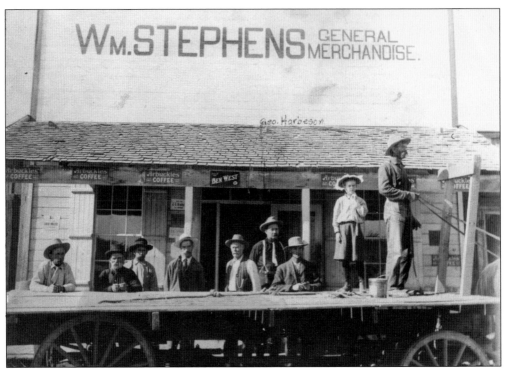

William Stephens operated a store on Main Street for several years, although the record is vague as to what years those were. The popular Camp Verde resident served as a county supervisor, was a partner in the ill-fated Verde Oil Company, and has his name cast in bronze on the dedication plaque of the historic county courthouse in Prescott.

Like several stores before it, the Kovacovich Mercantile store on Camp Verde's Main Street eventually lost its battle with the Wingfield Commercial Company. Owner Emil Kovacovich opened his first store in Cottonwood, eventually expanding to Jerome before opening his Camp Verde branch in the late 1920s. Kovacovich also had the Budweiser Beer distributorship for the valley.

One of the more famous buildings on Camp Verde's Main Street was the all-purpose building constructed by Fred Stephens and Bill Verden for owner Russ Mulholland. It was best known as Goswick Hall after Tom Goswick, the owner who bought it from Mulholland. The building hosted dances, movies, basketball games, and roller skating, and served as the community's de facto town hall. Today it is a business building housing a health food store, bookstore, and taxidermy shop.

There are only a handful of homes in town built from the native white limestone of the Verde Formation—formed by the sediments of an ancient lakebed. A classic example is the home of Boss Head, which like several of the other limestone buildings was built by Edwin C. Nursey, an English stone mason. Among the other buildings Nursey built were the James Henry Wingfield house and the Clear Creek Church.

Begun in 1898, the Clear Creek Church was completed in 1903. One of the valley's oldest surviving churches, it was constructed of white limestone quarried from the surrounding limestone hills. The parishioners placed a Bible and a $5 gold piece in the cornerstone when it was laid. Sometime in the 1920s, someone chiseled into the cornerstone. The culprit took the $5 gold piece but left the Bible. Abandoned as a church in 1912, the building served as a school until 1938. From World War II until 1949 it was a cannery serving area farmers. It eventually was owned by the Burgbacher family who, realizing its historical significance, donated it to the Camp Verde Historical Society in 1974. The historical society restored it between 1975 and 1979. Trudy Schilleman, wife of Elmer Schilleman, donated the original school bell in 1982. Elmer had acquired it when he bought the equipment from the cannery to use in his dairy.

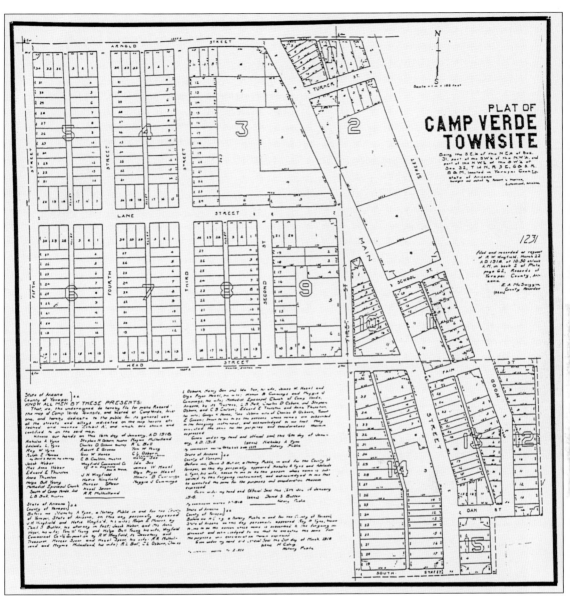

In 1918, a group of locals recorded a plat for the "Camp Verde Townsite." The plan laid out 225 lots in 15 irregular-shaped city blocks they hoped would sell for $25 to $250 each. The promoters believed that the railroad, which had just been built by copper mining mogul "Rawhide" Jimmy Douglas to his United Verde Extension Mine in Jerome, would soon reach Camp Verde, warranting some civic planning. Their dreams were dashed when copper prices collapsed after World War I and Douglas scrapped his plans to extend the railroad. Camp Verde did not get around to incorporating until 1986.

Known as the Green Building, one of the former enlisted men's barracks served the community for many years as a school. The building had two rooms and a basement. Margaret Wingfield Hallett, who began school when Camp Verde School District No. 28 held classes in the abandoned hospital of Fort Verde, once wrote that she remembered in third grade the students would go down to the basement and read letters and papers left by the soldiers. The building was used by the school district for a variety of purposes including a photographic darkroom, industrial arts shop, and a band room, until it was torn down in 1948.

The Camp Verde School District organized its first high school class in 1912, consisting of five students. Subjects taught were algebra, geometry, Spanish, English, and ancient history. A high school building was constructed in 1918 but burned in 1924. In 1948, Camp Verde voters passed a school bond, allowing for the construction of five new classrooms and a gymnasium.

Camp Verde School District 28 dates back to 1895–1896, but it was not until 1914 that the district had enough of a tax base to build its own schoolhouse. The building is constructed of native limestone laid by the district's school superintendent, G. W. Derrick. Today the old school building is owned by the Town of Camp Verde and leased to the Camp Verde Historical Society as its museum and research center.

Camp Verde's Main Street remained unpaved until the late 1960s. During winter 1967–1968, over 4 feet of snow packed the roads. When it melted, the roads turned to a sea of mud. The next year Main Street was paved. In 2004, when Arizona State Route 260 bypassed the town, the State of Arizona paid to have Main Street redone, complete with sidewalks, lighting, and landscaping.

In 1933, Claude and Ralph Wingfield decided to compete against their uncle, Robert Wingfield, and open a grocery. They went bust within a year. The building then became a cafe and, after prohibition, a bar. After a couple of rapid changes in ownership, Otto Boler and his partner, Orion "Hardluck" Southwick, purchased it in 1935. Hardluck, who had a brother named "Too Bad," soon sold out, and Boler eventually became the sole proprietor. Described by his son Bill as a "short fat Dutchman," Boler was not known for his customer service, gaining a reputation for concentrating on his own interest at the expense of his patrons. For instance, it was not until the 1950s and only when the female customers threatened to take their business to Cottonwood, that he purchased bar stools. When it closed in 2010, Boler's Bar was Camp Verde's longest continuously operating business.

Don and Gwen Gunnell purchased the burned out shell of a former café in 1965, renovated the building, and turned it into Don's Verde Burger Drive-In. From 1965 until long after the Gunnells sold the business, it was a popular eating place with area families, a hang out after sporting events, and a favorite stop for tourists. The Gunnells eventually expanded the building, partitioning it into the business suites that remain today.

A longtime favorite for many Camp Verdeans was Custard's Last Stand, a hamburger joint on Main Street. At various times during its heyday, it sold ice cream and baked goods, along with famous homemade candies and chocolates. Its signature horse on the roof was also a favorite of local pranksters who often roped it, dressed it in provocative lingerie, or gave it an occasional coat of paint. Today the building houses the Town of Camp Verde's Visitor Center .

The adobe building across the street from the old suttler's store, built by William "Boss" Head in 1883, has served the town in a variety of ways over its life. Originally it was a boardinghouse for travelers coming through town on the old Star Stage Line's stagecoach from Prescott. Most residents of Camp Verde still know it as the "Stage Stop." Over the years, it was also a residence, dressmaking shop, antique store, hotel, and even one of the town's earliest public libraries.

Six

THE STORE

It was a common practice for military posts to have a suttler, a civilian contractor who provided a wide variety of items not available through the military.

Two early settlers, Wales Arnold and Hugh Richards, filled that role initially. Then in 1870, Richards sold the business to Prescott businessman William "Boss" Head," although Richards remained at Camp Verde to manage the company.

In 1871, Head constructed an adobe building just outside the new fort. With it, he laid the cornerstone of what eventually became one of the longest continually operated businesses in Yavapai County history.

For years, Head's store was the one vestige of civilization in an otherwise remote and desolate country, providing farmers and ranchers with a wide variety of provisions as well as the accoutrements of the "outside" world.

A list of prices from the 1880s showed cigars could be purchased for $1 each, champagne for $2.50 a bottle, or a pair of boots for $10.

Head eventually sold the business to two young men from the community, Clinton Wingfield and Mac Rodgers. For the next few years, the two grew the business as well as their own reputations for honesty and hard work—until a stranger came out of the darkness on the night of July 2, 1899, and shot and killed both of them during a failed robbery.

The business passed on to Clinton Wingfield's father, James Henry Wingfield, who eventually traded it to his brother, William G. Wingfield, in 1909. In 1912, William's son Robert "Uncle Bob" Wingfield took over the store.

In 1918, Robert Wingfield incorporated the business as the Wingfield Commercial Company, a name it would keep for over 50 years. Loved and respected by the community, Robert Wingfield expanded the business while building a reputation for generosity that carried the business through the Great Depression, two world wars, and a devastating fire.

The store closed its doors in 1976, but the building remains standing, including the adobe walls laid by Boss Head.

Most of the walls of the old suttler's store, built in 1871, still stand. The building served as the only civilian structure on the nearly 10,000-acre Fort Verde Military Reservation and the center of public life for not only the military but the surrounding community of farmers and ranchers.

Wingfield's store not only served as Camp Verde's post office for many years, it also had many modern conveniences including a soda fountain and an ice plant. The gentleman on the right is Oliver Loper, store owner Robert Wingfield's cousin. The one on the left is Captain Smiley, a former Indian Scout for General George Crook and a well-known and loved fixture of the Camp Verde community for years.

On the evening of July 2,1899, the two young owners of the Wingfield-Rodgers store, Clinton Wingfield and Mac Rodgers, were killed by a solitary gunman as they were closing their store for the evening. Newspapers across the country, including the *Los Angeles Times* and the *New York Times*, covered the ensuing manhunt. On August 16, a New Mexico train robber by the name of Tom "Black Jack" Ketchum was arrested during a botched train robbery and eventually hung for his crime. Some of those who had been following the murderer's trail, including Yavapai County sheriff John Munds, believed Ketchum was the killer. However, there is no evidence Ketchum did it nor did he ever confess to the killings.

Following the murder of Clinton Wingfield and Mack Rodgers in 1899, Wingfield's father James Henry Wingfield bought Rodgers's interest from his widow. James Henry sold it to his brother William Gilmore in 1909, who was not very interested in running it. Three years later, after having tried several managers, William turned the business over to his son Robert, who turned it into the institution it was to become.

This picture of Robert Wingfield (left) was taken shortly after he began managing the store in 1912. The man on the right remains unidentified. Fifty years later, Wingfield noted that prices had changed little. In 1912, a 50-pound sack of sugar sold for $35, syrup was $4 a gallon, flour was $12 for 10 pounds, and a plug of tobacco sold for $1.

Robert Wingfield started working in the family business, the W. G. and R. W. Mercantile Company, in 1909, at a time when all the store's merchandise arrived via mule-drawn freight wagon, and whiskey was sold from a wooden cask for 12.5¢ (one bit) a shot. Always seen with a cigar in his mouth (though never lit), Uncle Bob expanded the business to include a bank, post office, icehouse, and butcher shop. The store sold just about everything, including Navajo rugs, shotgun shells, frozen pies, long-handled underwear, and saddles. Customers could also pay their phone and water bill, notarize a contract, or weigh a load of hay.

Most of the Wingfield Commercial Store's early business was done on credit. In those days, the extensive use of credit was necessary because the farmers and ranchers settled their accounts once a year when their crops were sold or their cattle went to market. There were several bad accounts on the company's ledger, not because the people were dishonest but because of hard times.

		WINGFIELD COMMERCIAL CO. CAMP VERDE, ARIZONA

M. Jno. S Boyn
Cherry, Ariz

STATEMENT OF YOUR ACCOUNT

For Mar 192 3

TERMS CASH.
Accounts are kept for the convenience of customers and are due on the first of the month.

WHOLESALE AND RETAIL DEALERS
GENERAL MERCHANDISE

Interest charged at the rate of 10% per annum on all past due accounts.

SAVE YOUR STORE TICKETS TO CHECK THIS STATEMENT

MADE BY BAKER-PRINTER CO. PA

PROOF			PURCHASED BY YOU		PAID ON ACCOUNT	BALANCE
1,501.31	MAR	9	BALANCE LAST. FORWARD 5 5			
1,510.51	MAR	12	.50	.60	5.00	
	MAR	12	.95	1.05	5.45	
1,524.06	MAR	21	1.90	.25	.50	
	MAR	21	3.50	2.25		
1,532.46	MAR	26	5.30	2.25	.40	
1,540.41	MAR	28	1.05			
1,541.46	MAR	31	1.25	7.70	3.20	
	MAR	31	.45	2.05	3.55	
1,559.66	MAR	31	52.50	.50	3.75	
1,616.61	APR	3	2.80	.50	3.00	
	APR	3	.25			
1,623.31	APR	6	1.83			
1,625.14	APR	11	8.10	7.80	2.25	
1,643.29	APR	14	13.10	2.85	2.25	
1,661.49	APR	19	6.35			
1,667.84	APR	26	.25	7.40	5.00	
	APR	26	1.71			
1,682.20	APR	30	3.15			
1,685.35	MAY	7	1.00	4.60	10.85	
1,701.80	MAY	12	4.45	5.50	2.25	
	MAY	12	2.85	.35	5.25	
	MAY	12	.60			
1,723.05	MAY	15	3.20			
1,726.25	MAY	17	3.90	2.20	1.80	
1,734.15	FEB	1	612.20 Bal carried from file			

Robert Wingfield eventually opened the Camp Verde National Bank in 1916 to round out his business empire. He kept it going until 1920, when one evening while he was out hunting, someone entered the back of the store and blew the vault door. The perpetrators were never found.

In 1917, residents of Camp Verde formed the Homeguards, not because they felt nervous about the Kaiser invading, but because they believed the Mexican bandit Pancho Villa was headed to the valley and may have wanted to rob the bank. Villa was rumored to be headed to Jerome, although there is no evidence he came anywhere close.

Like many of the families in Camp Verde, the Wingfields took advantage of the abandoned buildings at Fort Verde. Robert dismantled the fort's guardhouse and had it rebuilt behind the commercial store and used it to store hay. In 1910, the Wingfields hired Joseph Geimer, master mechanic for the Crystal Ice Company and the Arizona Brewing Company in Phoenix, to build a refrigeration plant and icehouse behind the commercial building.

A devastating fire burned through the Wingfield Mercantile Company store in 1940. The cause was never determined and much of the merchandise in the main store was destroyed. What was not destroyed was moved down the street to the former Kovacovich Building (Calvary Church today), and business resumed in less than 24 hours. Owner Robert Wingfield, whose stellar reputation and generosity had kept the business going through the Great Depression, was able to capitalize on that reputation after the fire. Residents drove to Phoenix to bring merchandise, and those with outstanding debts scraped together what they could to help "Uncle Bob" stay in business.

Like many members of Robert Wingfield's clan, his son Howard was raised in the store. One day while measuring a pair of Levis for Gertrude Cox, a young Flagstaff college student, he told her he was going to marry her. In 1927, she married Howard, much to the dismay of her family, who felt she should have at least finished her college education.

One of the store's biggest businesses was the sale of ammunition and fishing tackle. In this photograph, Camp Verde resident Ray Adams and his two sons Robert and Roy drop in to buy some lures from storeowner and fellow sportsman Howard Wingfield. Howard had a reputation for having the best up-to-date fishing and hunting news. However, it was a long-held family secret that he kept the best spots to himself.

The motto of the Wingfield Commercial Store was "Everything Under the Sun," reflecting a business model that kept the company going for over 80 years. Begun as a suttler's store, the business thrived as the farming community surrounding Fort Verde grew after the military left and the Jerome mines expanded. It closed its doors in 1976, two years after Howard Wingfield passed away.

Howard Wingfield sold Wingfield Commercial Company in 1971. Prior to closing its doors for the final time, it had a reputation for never having closed for more than 24 hours. The building was purchased in 2004 and restored into a commercial building with several business suites. Three of the adobe walls originally laid down in 1871 still stand.

Seven

THE MINES

Stories of mineral wealth in the Verde Valley go back centuries. Spanish maps from the early 1700s show Sierra Azul, the legendary "Blue Mountain" said to contain a king's ransom in gold and silver, located somewhere along the banks of the upper Verde River.

But long before the legends were first heard, before Spanish fortune hunters arrived, the Sinaguan people mined a deposit of salt left behind when an ancient freshwater lake dried up, located in what is now Camp Verde.

The Sinaguan miners tunneled through the relatively soft rock using stone tools, trading the salt for other goods, from around 900 A.D. until they mysteriously left around 1425.

In 1583, the Spanish search for the seven cities of Cibola and their streets of gold made its way to the Verde Valley in the person of Antonio de Espejo, a wealthy rancher and merchant. Espejo came looking for mines the Hopi said contained gold. Unimpressed with the copper ore he discovered, Espejo abandoned his search and returned home.

Other Spaniards came to visit but none stayed to work the mine. It was not until the 1880s that Americans working the blue-green ores discovered the mother lode.

The billion-dollar deposit of copper, gold, and silver, found beneath what would become the town of Jerome, would bring prosperity to the struggling farmers of Camp Verde. It would also cause others to explore the mountains closer to town for another deposit. Despite a search that still continues, that deposit has never been found. A brief oil rush that swept through Camp Verde around the turn of the 20th century also came up empty.

The Camp Verde salt mine operated intermittently from 1923 to 1933, producing a particular kind of salt used in the production of paper. The mine provided employment for as many as 100 men, most of them from the Camp Verde area, during some of the darkest days of the Great Depression. Cheaper imported salts eventually put the mine out of business.

In summer 1926, shovel operator Theodore Wingfield unearthed the mummy of an ancient miner at the American Products Company Salt Mine. The mummified body, which was eventually taken to the University of Arizona, may very well have been the oldest victim of an underground mining accident in North America. The Sinagua mined the deposit from around 900 to 1400 A.D.

The salt deposits found in Camp Verde resulted from the evaporation of an immense inland freshwater lake that once covered most of the Verde Valley. When the lake dried up, the minerals that saturated the lake water dropped out of solution, forming evaporite deposits. Along with the salt mine, Camp Verde also has an operating gypsum mine, which provides one of the key ingredients for the manufacture of cement at the cement plant in Clarkdale.

Camp Verde, along with much of the Verde Valley, sits atop the Verde Formation, a layer of freshwater lake sediments laid down between 10 million and 2.5 million years ago. The deposits have been measured at a depth of almost 2,000 feet beneath Camp Verde and at an elevation 1,300 feet above. First identified in 1923 by geologist A. O. Jenkins, the formation contains fossil remains and tracks of mastodons, saber-toothed tigers, and early ancestors of camels and horses.

The first oil well in the Verde Valley, during a brief oil frenzy that lasted from 1911 to 1913, was drilled on land owned by James Henry Wingfield. Owners of the Verde Oil Company, which included Wingfield and his partner William Stephens, found traces of oil but nothing in commercially viable quantities. The Verde Valley Oil Company's drill rig sold at a sheriff's auction in 1914.

The Verde Oil Company drilled a second well just north of its first one. A bit more aggressive than the first, the well went down 1,650 feet before the search ended. During the height of the oil rush, the hotel in Camp Verde was forced to put up tents along Main Street to handle all the speculators and hangers-on.

The man responsible for starting the Verde Valley oil boom was rancher Frank Turner. In early 1910, he began filing claims around Camp Verde, eventually enticing former business colleagues from Yuma into investing. By 1912, there were four companies drilling in the Verde Valley, including this rig located on Turner's ranch, owned by the Yuma-Verde Oil Company.

Soon after the Verde Valley's oil frenzy went bust, the investors' action moved up the Verde River to Chino Valley. United Chino Oil Company was one of a handful of companies that raised enough money to actually drill in Chino Valley. Four wells were sunk before the Chino Valley search ended.

Squaw Peak mine owner Edison Thacker spent 40 years trying to find the bonanza he believed lay beneath the east slopes of Squaw Peak, 5 miles south of Camp Verde. In spite of his best efforts, the mine never tapped into the rich vein Thacker believed was there. The only time the Squaw Peak Mine produced any measurable amount of ore was during World War II when the federal government generously subsidized its operating costs. In 1942, Thacker received a $20,000 loan from the Reconstruction Finance Corporation, a federal agency that was issuing loans to develop materials vital to the war effort. For a brief period, Thacker had a crew of 18 miners and a mule named Sheba, who reportedly worked a double shift. When the deep pockets of the Reconstruction Finance Corporation went empty in 1946, Thacker went out of business. (Graphic courtesy of Verde Valley Newspapers.)

It is said that Squaw Peak Mine owner Edison Thacker only came to town for two reasons—to buy groceries and sell stock. The mine incorporated in 1916 with Thacker as the president. Over the years, several Camp Verde residents were members of the company's board of directors including members of the Wingfield family and Otto Boler, owner of Boler's Tavern. A report written after the mine closed in 1946 stated that Thacker had issued 992,882 shares of $1 common stock and 3,000 shares of $100 preferred stock. In his defense, he dug over 4,000 feet of tunnels. Rumors of the big one often hit Camp Verde, and those with a little extra cash would get swept into the frenzy, always coming out on the short end. In the same report that listed the stock Thacker had sold, the state geologist speculated there was between $17 million and $187 million worth of copper and molybdenum in the mine.

The Squaw Peak Mine dates from the 1880s. L. M. Olden, a schoolteacher and lawyer turned miner, originally prospected the property. It is said that a lover jilted him sometime before he moved to Camp Verde. He eventually committed suicide.

Camp   Flotation mill   Shops and Tunnel Portal

The Squaw Peak Mine was the dream of Edison Thacker. Said to have been able to make almost anything run, Thacker lived, worked, and babied the mine. He died in 1956, his faith in the mine unshaken after operating it since 1918. Following his death, several multi-national mining companies, including Phillips Petroleum, spent millions exploring the mountain. It was last test drilled in 2008.

The mining community of Cherry served as the stopping point for travelers headed from Prescott into the Verde Valley. The town sits in a broad basin formed by Cherry Creek at an altitude of 5,500 feet. Many of the families that settled Camp Verde also had family in Cherry.

The Cherry Mining District, located in the Black Hills southwest of Camp Verde, contains many gold-bearing veins laced through the granite outcrops. The ore deposits are located within the Cherry Creek basin and also along a steep slope facing the Verde Valley.

Accommodations for the families of miners working in the Cherry Creek District were minimal, often consisting of a solidly constructed tent with a cook stove, kitchen table, and a bed. The transient lifestyle of miners did not afford the luxury of a permanent home, as the mines opened and shut at the whim of investors' dollars.

The Golden Idol Mine, also known as the Hillside Mine, was owned and operated by the Verde Inspiration Company and included a stamp mill and cyanide plant. During operations from 1906 to 1910, the ore was said to have contained $7 to $12 of gold per ton.

The Romance Mine was one of scores of mines located in the Cherry Mining District, south and west of Camp Verde. The Cherry mines extracted a respectable amount of gold, silver, and copper before the last of them closed after World War II.

Of all the mines in the Cherry Creek Mining District, none lasted as long as the Monarch. Also known as the Mocking Bird Mine, it opened in 1883 and was still producing commercially viable ores well into the 1920s. A report from the Arizona Bureau of Mines stated it was the richest mine in the Cherry Creek Mining District, averaging $20 per ton. Most all the mines in the district were gold mines, some producing ores that assayed in the $80 to $100 per ton range, although for brief periods, along with some silver.

Smelter smoke was a constant problem for all residents of the Verde Valley from the time the mines in Jerome went into high gear in the 1890s. However, it got considerably worse, especially for the farmers and ranchers, in 1913 when the United Verde Mine moved its smelter from Jerome to the valley floor. By the time the United Verde Extension Mine opened its smelter in Verde in 1918, an all-out battle was taking place between the ranchers and farmers and the mining companies. Mixed with rain, sulfur rich smelter smoke created sulfuric acid, ruining crops and destroying grassland. The legal battles and other disputes lasted until the UVX smelter closed in 1938.

In 1916, over 100 Verde Valley farmers and miners organized as the Verde Valley Protection Association to fight the United Verde and United Verde Extension. In response, the mining companies bought up the farms and ranches, then sold or leased them back with a "smoke easement" attached, preventing any further legal challenges over crop damage.

Eight

THE ARCHAEOLOGY

It has been argued that southwestern archaeology began at Camp Verde in fall 1865, with the arrival of Edwin Palmer. An English immigrant and army surgeon, as well as a frail and malaria-ridden plant collector, Palmer had asked for the assignment so he might broaden his interests in the natural world.

While out gathering snakes, lizards, and a variety of previously unidentified plants, Palmer discovered the remains of a previously unrecorded civilization. In comparing the preserved foodstuffs left behind, he was able to draw conclusions about Sinagua land use and cultivation practices. His work has also been described as the forerunner to the modern-day science of ethnobotany.

In 1884, a second military surgeon arrived at Fort Verde, whose fascination with the "monumental ruins" of an "extinct race of men," would draw others in his wake. An ornithologist by passion and medical doctor by training, Dr. Edgar Mearns spent four years scouring the ancient dwellings that littered the landscape. He is credited with discovering virtually every major pueblo within a 40-mile radius of Fort Verde, while collecting literally wagonloads of artifacts and sending them to eastern museums.

An article he wrote in 1890 for the well respected, if not so scholarly, *Popular Science Monthly*, entitled "Ancient Dwellings of the Rio Verde Valley," gave the region its first national exposure. It also sparked the interests of the first professional archaeologists to arrive, Cosmos Mindeleff and Jesse Walter Fewkes.

Mindeleff, an architect by training, mapped over 50 ruins along the Verde during a trip in 1891. A remarkable observer, his ability to interpret what he was seeing—land use patterns and settlement systems—was 75 years ahead of its time.

Fewkes, an ichthyologist turned ethnologist, came to the Verde in 1895. Accused of being an elitist snob as well as a plagiarist, Fewkes's real contribution was his belief in preserving the ancient dwellings and opening them to the general public.

Dr. Edgar Mearns was the surgeon at Fort Verde between 1884 and 1888. Although he wrote 125 scholarly papers on flora and fauna in his life, it was his paper on the ruins he encountered in his travels around Fort Verde, "Ancient Dwellings of the Rio Verde Valley," that brought him his first notoriety and the Verde Valley its first recognition for its rich trove of archaeological treasures.

Dr. Edgar Mearns spent much of his spare time excavating the ruins around the valley. He collected literally tons of pottery, stone tools, and other artifacts. Unfortunately for local archaeology, most of the artifacts were shipped elsewhere and few were logged as to where they were discovered.

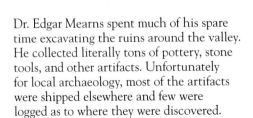

In 1891, a young surveyor and architectural model maker by the name of Cosmos Mindeleff was hired by the Bureau of American Ethnology to map and produce models of archaeological sites throughout the American Southwest. He mapped over 50 ruins on his survey from the Verde River's confluence with the Salt River to its confluence with Beaver Creek. His maps, drawings, and photographs are indicative of someone who had an eye for detail, and his surveys remain as accurate today as they were over 100 years ago. What also set him apart from his peers was his power of observation. He was one of the first in his field to write about environmental relationships and to attempt to interpret land use and settlement systems. (Graphic courtesy of Verde Valley Newspapers)

The earliest maps of the Verde Valley showed a mysterious water-filled cavity on Beaver Creek, just upstream from Camp Verde, known as Montezuma Well. The well is fed by a subterranean spring that drains into Beaver Creek. Its interior walls and surrounding landscape contain numerous cliff dwellings left by a culture that once called the desert oasis home. Early visitors believed it was Aztec in origin, thus the Montezuma label.

Fort Verde surgeon Dr. Warren Day was the first person to attempt measuring the depth of Montezuma Well. He gathered hundreds of feet of rope at Fort Verde, believing it was hundreds of feet deep. When he discovered it to be only about 65 feet deep, he soaked the rest of the rope, brought it back to the fort, and declared to all present that the well was "bottomless."

For all the curiosity about what lay beneath the surface of Montezuma Well, it was not until 1948, shortly after Montezuma Well became part of Montezuma Castle National Monument, that someone dove to the bottom. Upon surfacing, diver H. J. Charbonneau confirmed what famous newspaperman Charles Lummis had speculated some 60 years earlier, specifically that the well was "a creepy place." Charbonneau reported that he had gone down 50 feet before encountering a bottom of swirling fine silt. He also said that the pond was thick with leeches starting at 30 feet down and that he stepped on "something soft, slimy, and large," which caused him great concern. There have been nine documented dives to the bottom since Charbonneau's dive. The most recent one, made by a team of divers from the National Park Service's Submerged Resources Center, determined the spring that feeds the well enters through two vent holes, one of which measured 137 feet deep and the other 193 feet deep.

Until it became part of Montezuma Castle National Monument in 1947, Montezuma Well was privately owned. The Back family, owners of the property, had a private museum and would take visitors for boating trips around the lake.

The rim of Montezuma Well is laced with the ruins of ancient homes that were once occupied by the Sinagua people. The well and the surrounding area was inhabited from 1100 to 1425. A relatively advanced culture, the Sinagua diverted the outlet of the well into a canal and irrigated acres of farmland along Beaver Creek.

The first Americans to visit the Verde Valley were two fur trappers led by legendary southwestern trapper Ewing Young. Unfortunately for modern historians, Young kept no record of his travels. Nevertheless, it is believed that he or members of his trapping company were the first to see Montezuma Castle, located 7 miles north of Fort Verde on the banks of Beaver Creek.

One of the best-preserved and better-known cliff dwellings in the Southwest is Montezuma Castle. Also one of the valley's first tourist attractions, it became America's first national monument in 1906, shortly after Congress passed the Antiquities Act.

Whether or not the Spanish expeditions of Antonio Espejo, Marcus Farfan, or Don Juan de Onate, in the late 16th and early 17th centuries, saw Montezuma Castle is a matter of speculation. However, chroniclers of the expeditions did note the many "pueblos" in the area.

Custodian Earl Jackson began his career at the castle in 1925, the 15-year-old son of Martin Jackson, the castle's first custodian. Earl Jackson became the first full-time employee three years later. He would later receive a master's degree in archaeology at the University of Arizona before being hired as the monument's custodian upon his father's retirement in January 1937.

Montezuma Castle celebrated the dedication of a new visitor center in September 1950. The visitor center and museum is a 2,500-square-foot facility that includes a lobby, exhibit rooms, offices, and a paved patio. The visitor center replaced the Jackson family home that had served as a museum and offices since 1926. (Photograph courtesy of National Park Service)

Montezuma Castle requires a considerable degree of maintenance to keep it from falling down. At one time, visitors were welcome to walk through the facility, a practice that is now limited to those who have a reason to be there. Here a National Park Service worker applies a coat of sealer to the roof of the uppermost room.

The countryside in and around Camp Verde is replete with petroglyphs—ancient figures and symbols chipped into the rock. Some petroglyph sites, such as the panels at V Bar V Heritage Site, just north of Camp Verde, are covered with over 1,000 objects, including geometric, plant, and animal figures. Some are thought to be elements of solar calendars. Most however, remain a mystery.

Many ancient dwellings have been discovered in the Verde Valley. The vast majority of sites were looted of valuable artifacts long before professional archaeologists ever had a chance to interpret the stories they could tell and long before laws were in place to protect them.

Nine

THE OTHER STUFF

With its cowboys and Indians, its fort and families, and its countryside and characters, Camp Verde is a treasure trove of history. Its history is more than big events or the larger than life players who shaped the valley—it is a tapestry of private lives, celebrations of life, wild ideas, and simple folks, many of whom lived their lives outside the spotlight.

Like everywhere else, it has had its share of charlatans, scoundrels, and bootleggers. But it has also had more than its share of decent hardworking people just looking for a simpler life.

Over the years, Camp Verde has dodged more than one bullet aimed its way and managed to come out no worse for the wear.

It had its own movie star. It has a meteorite that bears its name. And it sits amid a landscape of spectacular beauty.

This last chapter wraps up some of those loose ends in an attempt to show that Camp Verde is probably no different than any other small town in America, while at the same time, displaying a remarkable uniqueness.

The community of Aultman once stood at the junction of the Cherry Road and the road from Camp Verde to Jerome. Aultman had a post office from 1885 to 1907, with one brief interruption between 1890 and 1892, when the post office and store burned down. In its time, the community sported a general store, gas station, school, and a post office. Camp Verde businessman Robert Wingfield met his wife while working at the Aultman store. The town was abandoned in 1923. Today the townsite that was Aultman has been incorporated into the town limits of Camp Verde.

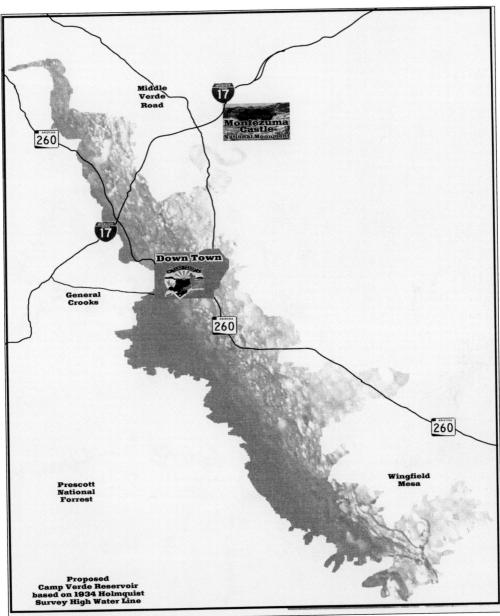

The map includes the following labels:

Middle Verde Road

INTERSTATE 17

ARIZONA 260

Montezuma Castle National Monument

INTERSTATE 17

Down Town

General Crooks

ARIZONA 260

ARIZONA 260

Wingfield Mesa

Prescott National Forrest

Proposed Camp Verde Reservoir based on 1934 Holmquist Survey High Water Line

A proposed dam 10 miles south of Camp Verde would have submerged most of the town beneath a 15-mile-long reservoir—had it been built. Instead, at the last minute, the dam and the irrigation project it was meant to serve was denied funding by the Bureau of Reclamation. Known as the Paradise Verde Project, backers had planned to divert water from the Verde River to irrigate several thousand acres in north Phoenix—that is, before a feasibility study showed it was too costly and that flows of the Verde River were inadequate to meet demand. According to the high water survey, the lake would have come to the front steps of what is now the Camp Verde Historical Society Museum. (Courtesy of Verde Valley Newspapers.)

The coming of the territorial highway, a road running from Douglas to the Grand Canyon, in 1911, brought with it the first bridge over the Verde River. After lobbying by other communities in the valley, including Cherry and Aultman, the state chose a route down Copper Canyon, through Camp Verde, and across the river at a location just upstream from its confluence with Wet Beaver Creek. The Missouri Valley Bridge and Iron Company built the 300-foot span. Known as Black Bridge, the iron structure stood for over 60 years before a new concrete span was built in 1974.

The second bridge over the Verde River was built in 1935, after a good deal of controversy. The State of Arizona pushed to build the bridge on the road to Fossil Creek, as private interests were planning to build a dam. The dam promoters claimed the bridge plans undermined their ability to sell bonds. The original two-lane bridge was widened to four lanes in 2004.

Just outside Camp Verde in Cottonwood Basin stand some unusual rocks known locally as the Tee Pee rocks. They are called fumaroles and were formed by steam escaping when volcanic ash from the Hackberry Volcano fell across an ancient fresh water lake that once covered the floor of the Verde Valley. The calcium-rich waters of the lake were heated by the ash, creating a form of natural cement, which when exposed due to the erosion of the surrounding ash created the unusual formations. The pock-marked holes are the result of water eroding the cones as they slowly exposed themselves to the elements. The Hackberry Volcanic field was active between 2.2 million and 3.9 million years ago. It was initially believed that lava flows from the volcano created a dam that impounded the ancient lake; however, it is now believed the lake was caused by the slow subsidence of the valley floor over millions of years.

Sometime in the 1920s, a Phoenix pothunter named George Dawson discovered a sandstone cistern inside an ancient ruin just east of Camp Verde. When he pulled back the lid of the cistern, he found a feather blanket, inside of which was an iron meteorite. Dawson kept the meteorite for several years, eventually selling it to the world famous meteorite collector H. H. Nininger. Known to this day as the Camp Verde Meteorite, it is housed at Arizona State University's Center for Meteorite Studies. It is believed to be a fragment of the Canyon Diablo Meteorite, the one that created Arizona's famous Meteor Crater outside Winslow. How the 135-pound fragment made its way to the Verde Valley, 75 miles south, and how or why it ended up wrapped in a feather blanket and stowed away in an ancient Indian ruin, remains a mystery. (Courtesy of Verde Valley Newspapers.)

A diorama on display at the Cline Library at Northern Arizona University shows how the Camp Verde area may have looked a million years ago when it was home to saber-toothed cats, mastodons, and early relatives of the horse and camel. A handful of mastodon sites have been discovered over the years, including a spectacular set of tusks found 20 miles west of Camp Verde in the limestone quarry of a cement plant. The tusks were discovered when a student from Northern Arizona University spotted an ivory tooth sticking out of the ground while having lunch during a field trip. Within the town limits of Camp Verde are several sets of footprints left in the shores of an ancient lake.

Beginning in 1927, a group of valley pioneers began to meet once or twice a year for what became known as the Pioneer Picnic. In spite of a 12-year hiatus, the Pioneer Picnic is still held annually, making it the oldest community event in the valley.

Over the last 53 years, Fort Verde Days has played host to more than its share of dignitaries. Here well-known Verde Valley rancher Jess Goddard pours a cup of coffee for former Arizona governor and former U.S. secretary of the interior, Bruce Babbitt.

Camp Verde's biggest blowout of the year has been Fort Verde Days, ever since the Fort Verde Museum Association started it in 1957. The celebration, which includes a parade and numerous other events, celebrates the town's deep ties to the historic fort it grew up around.

The Fort Verde Days parade, first held in 1958, was originally split into two parades—one for all horse-drawn or horseback entries and one for everyone else. Today the parade, which lasts for most of an hour, draws entrants from the surrounding communities and throughout northern Arizona.

As with all small town parades, the Fort Verde Days parade includes its fair share of silliness and frivolity.

Along with its frivolity, Fort Verde Days and its parade have never been known for political correctness. This float from the 1965 Fort Verde Days shows a minister holding services over the grave of a pioneer, presumably killed by Indians, while a cavalry officers stands triumphantly over the body of a slain Indian.

Ever since 1960, the town has anointed one of its debutantes as the Colonel's Daughter. The young woman serves as the town's ambassador of goodwill during the Fort Verde Day celebration. The Camp Verde Cavalry sponsors the Colonel's Daughter pageant each year. (Courtesy of Verde Valley Newspapers.)

The Town of Camp Verde has long had a reputation as a place that never misses an opportunity to celebrate. As a result, the town has several festivals, including a Pecan Wine and Antique Festival, celebrating the local wineries and pecan farms, Cornfest, which celebrates the town's famous sweet corn, and a Crawdad Festival that celebrates the fresh water lobster that inhabit local streams and irrigation canals. (Courtesy of Verde Valley Newspapers.)

There are few people in Camp Verde's long history who have spent as much time gathering and publishing stories from the community's past as Florence Dickinson. Along with the writing she did for the Camp Verde Historical Society, she was a regular contributor to the *Verde Independent* history column, "Those Were the Days." Many of her stories were first hand accounts related to her by the old timers—accounts that might otherwise have been lost to time.

Around 1917, just after his first wife passed away, George Hance built a new home for his new wife, Evelyn Grace. There is some question as to whether or not the two ever took possession, as their marriage was very short lived. Today the building is owned by the Camp Verde Historical Society and is opened to the public for tours and on special occasions.

Although movie stars often vacationed at the dude ranches around Camp Verde to escape the limelight of Hollywood and relax, only one of them made it their home, cowboy western movie star Leland "Tumble" Weed. Weed, whose real name was Bob Baker, originally beat out Roy Rodgers for a coveted "B" western movie contract offered by Universal Studios. After retiring in 1944, Weed moved to Prescott, where he joined the police force, and eventually to Camp Verde to become a well-known saddle maker.

Prohibition may have made the manufacture and sale of alcohol a crime, but the Great Depression, ample water, and remoteness made it a cottage industry throughout the Camp Verde Area. Ed Dugan, owner of the Bull Pen Ranch, reportedly ran one of the largest moonshine operations in the Verde Valley, selling "Dugan's Dew," across the valley and across social classes.

In summer 1912, Camp Verde resident Blanche Casner won a trip to Los Angeles for selling newspaper subscriptions. On a boat trip across the harbor, she was "met, wooed, won and wed," in the course of four days, by San Diego resident and marine engineer William C. Canton. The newspapers stated that Miss Casner, "a veritable daughter of the hills," was 18 years old, but her friends and family in Camp Verde knew she was just 16. Asked what her parents might think of the marriage, she was quoted as saying, "I don't know what mama will say, but I guess she won't make too big a fuss. We will go and see her sometime." Mr. Canton would be the first of four husbands Blanche would "woo" in her lifetime.

ABOUT THE
ORGANIZATION

The Camp Verde Historical Society began in 1954 when the Camp Verde Improvement Association undertook the restoration of old Fort Verde. The scope of the project called for the organization of a committee, which became the Fort Verde Museum Association. Short of adequate funding to purchase the remaining building and the parade grounds, the association sold Fort Verde to the State of Arizona on August 17, 1970. In 1971, with the Museum Association's work completed, the organization changed its corporate name to the Camp Verde Historical Society.

Today the society has approximately 200 members. It owns two properties, the Clear Creek Church and the George Hance House. It also owns the rights to *Pioneer Stories of Arizona's Verde Valley*, a book of firsthand accounts of the early pioneers first published in 1933.

Camp Verde Historical Society
435 South Main Street
P. O. Box 1184
Camp Verde, Arizona 86322
(928) 567-9560

www.arcadiapublishing.com

Discover books about the town where you grew up, the cities where your friends and families live, the town where your parents met, or even that retirement spot you've been dreaming about. Our Web site provides history lovers with exclusive deals, advanced notification about new titles, e-mail alerts of author events, and much more.

MADE IN THE USA

Arcadia Publishing, the leading local history publisher in the United States, is committed to making history accessible and meaningful through publishing books that celebrate and preserve the heritage of America's people and places. Consistent with our mission to preserve history on a local level, this book was printed in South Carolina on American-made paper and manufactured entirely in the United States.

This book carries the accredited Forest Stewardship Council (FSC) label and is printed on 100 percent FSC-certified paper. Products carrying the FSC label are independently certified to assure consumers that they come from forests that are managed to meet the social, economic, and ecological needs of present and future generations.

FSC
Mixed Sources
Product group from well-managed forests and other controlled sources

Cert no. SW-COC-001530
www.fsc.org
© 1996 Forest Stewardship Council

Find Your Place in History.